# YOUR IDENTITY

## THE THUMBPRINT OF GOD

# YOUR IDENTITY

## THE THUMBPRINT OF GOD

*Dr. Mark D. White*

Unless otherwise noted, Scripture quotations are taken from
THE KING JAMES BIBLE.

GOD'S WORD Translation (GW)
Copyright © 1995 by God's Word to the Nations. Used by permission of Baker Publishing Group

Amplified Bible (AMP)
Copyright © 1954, 1958, 1962, 1964, 1965, 1987 by The Lockman Foundation

ISBN-13: 978-1508547983
ISBN-10: 150854798X

Printed and Manufactured in the United States

For additional copies of this book and other resources,

contact Dr. Mark D. White by email: rapha@gmx.us or zdkadar@gmail.com

Page and Cover design:  C. Rayne Warne – rainydaypictures@gmail.com

I want to say thank you to Theresa Nichols whose help will always be very much appreciate...

# DEDICATION

*This book is dedicated to my Dad, Rev. James H. White Jr.
my Mother Anna Mae White.  My three wonderful
children Seth Aaron, Jordan Austin
and Micah Anna Grace*

*All of you which have helped keep me on course
for the purpose of the Kingdom of our Lord Jesus Christ.
I love you and bless you!*

*Thank you Jesus, for you have not finished in me what you have
started, But you watch over your word to fulfill it in me.*

# CONTENTS

# Introduction

The life we have been called to live can be greatly affected and diminished by the imposed mindset which can be created by family, friends and situations. Who you are and who you are created to be has purpose to affect lives and all creation. As stated in Isaiah 64:8, "But now, LORD, You are our Father. We are the clay, and You are our potter. We are the work of Your hands. (GWT)

Life is full of opportunities to succeed or to fail. So, when your foundation (what you believe about yourself) is established on someone who believes in you, then consistency of pursuit is the subconscious drive which keeps you going because of the personal connection and the power of agreement. Life is full of challenges, opportunities with pressures to compromise, to quit and even hand off responsibilities to another.

Your life that is given is established with faith in you stated in Galatians 3:20, we are to live based on the faith of the Lord Jesus Christ who has great expectancy in your self-motivation, committed integrity, with overwhelming patience to never give up.

We are our Creator's creation, but if you have accepted Jesus as Lord and Savior, you are A Father's child that has the DNA, divine nature and ability of your redeemer, Jesus Christ!

Each chapter addresses issues of compliance and adaptation which are laid out for you. Going through life you have been challenged or defeated or even wounded emotionally. . Life goes on while the moon never sets. The sun always shines somewhere on this planet. No matter what it looks like or feels like, you can start over and over till you win in your eyes. Micah 7:8 says, "Rejoice not over me my enemy, for when I fall, I shall arise." Seeing yourself with the eyes of Jesus means you declare your future and fight to not repeat your past.

## Chapter 1

# The Creator of Heaven & Earth Knows Who You Are!

Thousands of years before a man named Jesus Christ was born, clay pottery was made and sealed with a potter's finishing touch. Before the fire finished the vessel, the thumb print of the potter was placed on the finished item as a signature of work. Vessels were made for use in homes in storing water, oil or food. In the finish work of the vessel, it was put to the heat to secure its shape and purpose. The last thing the potter would do was to place his thumbprint on the vessel for identity purposes signifying who made the vessel.

**You are more than your very physical DNA**

This book is a comparison to the lives of people around the

world as their lives were shaped and influenced by God during bad or good times. What is so wonderful is to comprehend how special you are in God's eyes, not even knowing you have His thumbprint on your life. You are more than your very physical DNA (deoxyribonucleic acid: the molecular basis of one's heredity) which is everything that makes you who you are. Your voice print, your distinction and details of your finger prints, or even the iris of your eyes all can identify you. But if you have been born again, His DNA (God's Divine, Nature and Attributes) is working inside you to change you into His image. This process starts at when you accepted Jesus as your Lord.

It is within your reach to know Him personally and to know how much He loves you.. God really wants you to have understanding and to see and understand the extra care He has taken to cause your life to grow toward the destiny which He has chosen for you. You having the knowledge of His perfect will at times seems beyond the reach of stars in the heaven. You are very special in the eyes of God. But, how you see yourself is what He is working to change. How you respond in the everyday aspect of your life on this planet earth is affected by ones self-image.

## Life is what you make it; you make it yourself

Life seems at times to be escalating or speeding things up as situations cause changes to take place in our daily lives. This happens as change begins and ends in our minds while yielding to or resisting ones emotions or response to situation. This brings one to creating their future or recreating their own past.

Our response in everyday life is the difference from being strong and secure compared to emotional and troubled while giving place to worry that is mixed with fear. It's like trained unconscious skills of karate, boxing or self-defense skills. These subconscious skills are like a response of one's tomorrow. When something happens unsuspectingly; our response is built on what is in our makeup or character, culture, upbringing, second nature and disciplined attributes.

The triad of who we are in this life is so much like the person God is. We are a spirit; We have a soul, We live in a body (I Thessalonians 5:23). We are created in His image. God is Father, God the Son, and God the Holy Spirit. Three, but yet one, so is all of humanity. Three is the display of our lives; past, present, and future. All are divided but yet one. We are divided within ourselves, confused and at times troubled. Truth is one issue that over a period of time will speak up from the ashes of corruption no matter what you have experienced.

Life is what you make it; you make it yourself. I am not talking

NOTES

_____

_____

_____

about how you live as much as how you respond to life experiences. It is your response that makes you a winner even if you lose during life at times. No matter the moment, will you keep trying?

## No matter the moment, will you keep trying?

In the midst of your daily choices are the hands of God still shaping your reasoning into the wonderful individual you are. As time progresses, one day you see the investment in your life which took place over a period of time. He said He would never leave you and to me that means He will never leave me the way I am or my situation the way it is. Developing trust and faith in someone is based on the relationship. As the relationship grows, trust increases.

Years ago while I was investing time in fasting and prayer, the Word of the Lord came to me with this understanding. He said no matter how small or big, how simple or profound, if something is important to His children, it's important to Him and for me to make it important to myself. To know His love is to know how much He loves you! We are more than creation. We are family, the children of God if you have accepted Jesus Christ as your Lord and savior.

—————————————— NOTES ——————————————

_____

_____

_____

16

The Apostle Paul wrote in the second letter to his spiritual son, Timothy, instructing him to study and apply himself to be favored by God. Any good parent will take notice of the choices of each child. The response of a good father or mother is based on the good or bad choices of each child. Even if bad choices were made, the love of good parents never stops. God is love and he will never stop loving you, me or anyone else (I John 4:7, 8).

In Hebrews chapter 4, verse 12, the scripture tells us that the Word of God gives distinction to the spirit, soul, and our body. This is the triad in us as it is in God, which gives distinction and clarity in our identity. The only way the three can become one is by the power of agreement. Ecclesiastes states that a threefold cord is not easily broken (Eccl. 4:12). As I quoted I Thessalonians 5:23, "We are a spirit; we have a soul, and live in a body" which God wants to preserve blameless and pure to do His works on earth.

I remember leaving a church service one day years ago and we had a strong move of Gods power. Healings and miracles took place. A deaf ear was healed and a blind eye was opened. The pastor rebuked me after service and told me even though God used me in miracles, I did not preach in love. I submitted to his words and left pondering. As I drove several miles I began crying before the Lord in prayer. I pondered my message and how I de-

---

NOTES

_____

_____

_____

17

livered it, I was broken that I was misunderstood by that pastor.

## Relationships come with influence

All at once the Word of the Lord came to me and said "Mark, not only do I love you, I like you." The impression was so strong on what the Spirit of God said to me that I had to pull off the road and stop driving because of the flowing tears of joy. I understand the principle, you can love someone from a distance, but you hang around or spend a lot of time with the people you like. That blew me away that God liked hanging with me.

When I asked Jesus to be my Lord and live in my heart at the age of seven in West Monroe, Louisiana at my Dads church Southside Assembly of God. It was on New Year's Eve 1964, my spirit was born again. My soul, which is my mind will and emotions, was not born again. I still deal with negative thoughts at times, bad tempting feelings at times, which by choice I can change by doing God's Word. As I grow older in this world, my body changes and my mind takes in knowledge. But without my spirit being born again, there is no opportunity to know God. I can know about Him, but to have a day-to-day relationship is impossible without receiving Jesus Christ as Lord of my life and daily seeking to know Him.

--------------------------------- NOTES ---------------------------------

_____

_____

_____

Relationships come with influence and understanding. A relationship is an investment that guarantees a mutual return. Even Proverbs says for a man to have friends he must show himself friendly. (Proverbs 18:24). It's the shed blood of Jesus that has opened all of Heaven to be made available to people like you and me. When I asked Jesus to come in my heart, this was the beginning of having an understanding of my purpose and destiny in this life. Jesus said, "Seek and you will find, ask and it will be given, knock and the door will open." This is all about a relationship with God.

Proverbs states, "As a man thinks, his lifestyle is created by the same." The power of your words affects not only you, but also people around you. There is life and death in your words. (Proverbs 18:21). Matthew 10:12 says, "out of the abundance of the heart the mouth speaks." The fruit of your lips comes from the seed of your thoughts. To please or meet my parents' approval, the effort is in doing in character how they have raised me. My character is the display of my own self-worth and trust that others can have in me.

In 2nd Timothy verse 19 of chapter 2, the bold declaration is made, "The foundation of God stands sure, knowing this; the Lord knows those that are His." Exodus 32:26 asks the question, "Who is on the Lord's side?" In the difficult times of life, a

—————————————————————— NOTES ——————————————————————

_____

_____

_____

strong relationship is committed no matter the outcome. God is faithful. He cannot lie. He will never leave you. He answers your desire for help in moments of need.

The Holy Spirit knows how to work with individuals, one on one, to bring about the perfect will of God in their lives. In 2nd Corinthians 3:18, Paul describes the steps of growth as having levels from glory to glory. Galatians 3:25 makes the same insinuation about growth. There are steps from childhood to adulthood. Growth requires management. Whether gardens, children, animals, finances, health, even cooking all requires oversight.

Responsibility and accountability are a part of success. Mandates are made for goals, visions and desired results. To whom much is given is much required. Luke 12:48, "For unto whomsoever much is given, of him shall be much required: and to whom men have committed much, of him they will ask the more". The verse in 2nd Timothy 19 states in finishing part of the verse, "and let everyone that names the name of Christ, depart from iniquity." Iniquity is an attitude of independence which says, I am going to do what I want to do, no matter the consequences.

## Responsibility and accountability are a part of success

The prophet Isaiah speaks concerning the thoughts of God are

——————————————— NOTES ———————————————

_____

_____

_____

not like ours, and neither are His ways like our ways. The way we do things has the influence of this earth. God is perfect and His way is perfect. He has given the Holy Spirit to live in us, and guide us into the changes that bring perfection. See and understand what Isaiah was saying in Isaiah 55 verses 8 and 9. "For as the heavens are higher than the earth, so are my ways higher than your ways and my thoughts **higher** than your thoughts." The way that the Father God looks at life somewhat different than the way most people look at it. The Father God's whole perspective is based on the law of sowing and reaping based on what He sowed and then what we sow.

## You don't have any problems; all you need is faith in God.

There are people that try to pull you down with their words and actions toward you. Now think, look down at what is under your feet which is dirt. People of this earth, also called carnal, pull you down to their level. Like the earth pulls you down with gravity. But we are not of this world. We are of a new Heaven and a new Earth. Because of the blood of Jesus, we are the redeemed of the Lord. God's thoughts about you are not in agreement with the status quo. That is why He believes in you so much and loves you no matter what you have done. He gave His Son for your future. As the blood of Jesus coveres your repented past. **God**

———————————————— NOTES ————————————————

_____

_____

_____

has created you a brand new **future, a brand new** tomorrow. Love believes the best and love protects what it loves. God's hand is on you. He has put His thumbprint on your life as He shapes **your** tomorrow inside of you.

He uses what the devil means for your hurt or destruction and turns it around for your good. Your identity in God's eyes is different than in your eyes or your family's eyes. Acts 1:7 makes a comment that God reserves the right to control times and seasons. He can change things in moments. A prophetess friend of mine named Patty reminds me that all it takes to change a life is one check, one phone call or one letter. As Kenneth Copeland states, "One word from God can change your life forever". R. W. Shambach says, "You don't have any problems; all you need is faith in God."

## Gods thoughts toward you lines up with the nature of God

In the book of Galatians chapter 6 verse 7, the principle of God is established in simple words. "Be not deceived; God is not mocked: For whatsoever man sows that shall he also reap". "God is not mocked" or taken lightly; this means that whatever you give out is what you have coming back to you. Your tomorrow would be a by-product of your today, if it wasn't for the grace of

———————————————— NOTES ————————————————

_____

_____

_____

God. 1st Peter 4:8 tells you that love covers a multitude of sins. First John 4:8 simply puts it that if you know God, you love like God. God is love.

You are unconditionally loved, believed in and invested in. You have a future and a hope as stated in Jeremiah 29:11. God's thoughts toward you line up with the nature of God, God is love, and love believes the best, endures long, takes no account of evil done to it and never rejoices over injustice. This is the process of the working of the Holy Spirit. He wants to lead you to the way of victorious living from inside out.

The Lord knows those who are His. He knows your name, your birthday, your weakness and strengths. He even knows the number of hairs on your head (Mathew 10:30) or even the real color of your hair. He knows your thoughts and even understands your actions. He knows because He bore your grief's and carried your sorrows to the cross, where He died. So, let us accept the fact that He also knows what to expect out of you on a daily basis.

He knows what investments are in you and what your abilities are. He knows what your hopes and dreams are. He knows what your level of faith is and knows what your level of obedience is or should be. He that is the Alpha and Omega; He is the beginning and the end, He knows all sees all and allows you to have a say

──────────────── NOTES ────────────────

_____

_____

_____

in your future. Our God is so awesome!

Galatians 2:20 "I am crucified with Christ
In Mathew 8:10, Jesus describes great faith, Then in Mathew 8:26, He describes little faith. Hebrews 11:6 tells us that without faith you can't please God. Faith is the attitude you maintain about the faithfulness of God, because if He said it that settles it. Time is your friend and negative fearful thoughts are your enemy. The responsibility is on us. We are to respond to our ability that the God of Heaven and Earth has given us with His Word and Spirit.

In 1st John 4:4, it speaks of the greater one that is in you, that being the Holy Spirit.  Someone saying you can't believe or hope in God, does not line up with what God says about you. Philippians 4:13 says you can do all things through Christ who enables you. Jesus told a man after He touched his eyes to heal his blindness, "Be this according to your faith." Your faith and my faith is an expectancy of agreement with God's Word. Your will allows an attitude that is an issue of compliance or defiance concerning the conversations of God. Amos 3 asks the question "How can two walk together without agreement?" This clearly agrees with the statement that a house divided has destiny to crumble and fall.

———————————————  NOTES  ———————————————

——————————————————————————————————————

——————————————————————————————————————

——————————————————————————————————————

Know this "God only inspects what He expects." There is a responsibility on our part to examine ourselves and judge ourselves so that we are not judged (1st Corinthians 11:31). To examine ourselves is to see if we are in the faith of our Lord Jesus, what Jesus believes for you. Hebrews 7:25 says he lives to pray for you. Galatians 2:20 instructs us "to live by the faith of our Lord Jesus Christ." It is His faith in His Word in you, His will for you; better yet His hand on your life that is helping you shape your tomorrow. His thumbprint on you is your identity. Your personality, your appearance, is all in His hand. He is working with you to shape your future while He erases your past.

No matter what seems not right in your life the hand of God is at work in your life. He once told me to look at the trees, so reluctantly I did. At the time my life really seemed messed up. As I was doing what I was instructed, the wind began to blow the leaves and the trees began to bend in the direction of the wind. Then the word of the Lord came to me, "What you cannot see is moving what you see." This made me realize that nothing is hopeless; God is still at work in your life, so keep the faith in His faithfulness.

**God does not waste words, time or power!**

Colossians 1:16 tells us "For by him were all things created, that

———————————— NOTES ————————————

_____

_____

_____

are in heaven, and that are in earth, visible and invisible, whether they be thrones, or dominions, or principalities, or powers: all things were created by him, and for him: And he is before all things, and by him all things consist." Understand the purpose of all the detail and scripture after scripture is important to your foundation. To know Jesus is to know His Word. To know God is to know His Word. To know your future is to know His Word. Knowing the Word of God helps keep you from being deceived or mislead. Trusting government leaders is okay, but trusting your Pastor is required. But if anyone takes you away from the Word of God, Paul said in Galatians 1:9, if anyone discredits the Word of God let him be accursed or judged severely.

Your identity is in this verse of Galatians 2:20, "I am crucified with Christ: nevertheless I live; yet not I, but Christ liveth in me: and the life which I now live in the flesh I live by the faith of the Son of God, who loved me, and gave himself for me." This means that Jesus has hope and expectancy for me and in me. That means we have a destiny, which is the will of God for our lives **to affect other peoples lives.**

His will is not to fail, or be sick, **not to** be poor or distraught in our emotions. But to have expectancy **which** lines up with God's will concerning your **life.** Second Corinthians 2:14 decrees that we give thanks unto God, who always causes us to

———————————  NOTES  ———————————

_____

_____

_____

triumphant causing the atmosphere to be filled with the acknowledgement of God Jehovah (not Allah) everywhere.

Remember these words; God does not waste words, time or power! He invests in what He believes in. He believes in you. The potter is shaping the clay; while the outcome of your life has the thumbprint of God imbedded in it. Isaiah 64:8 boldly speaks of Gods involvement in your life, "But now, O LORD, thou art our father; we are the clay, and thou our potter; and we all are the work of thy hand".

Archaeologist have found vessels of clay from five thousand B.C. which still had a detailed impression of the potter's pristine thumbprint clearly pressed against the bottom of the vessel. This being a signature seal of approval on a clay vessel made by a potter. This signature seal of approval is on your life. God has given to you the earnest down payment of Heaven, this being the gift and person of the Holy Spirit.

The indwelling of the Holy Spirit is for the purpose of leading you, teaching you and establishing an understanding of what potential is inside of you, because of Jesus. Ephesians 3:20 gives the understanding of what God has placed in you after your new birth in His Kingdom. "Now unto him that is able to do exceeding abundantly above all that we ask or think, accord-

_____ NOTES _____

_____

_____

_____

27

ing to the power that works in us." The following verses even more establish the concept of the greatness of "Christ in you the hope of Glory." (Colossians 1:27).

The book of Philippians in chapter 1 verse 6 gives understanding of the commitment of God toward you. "Being confident of this very thing, that He which hath begun a good work in you will perform it until the day of Jesus Christ:" Philippians 2:13, "For it pleased God which works in you both to will and to do of His good pleasure." I really love this one, Psalms 138:8, "The Lord will perfect that which concerns me; thy mercy, O Lord, endures forever; forsake not the work of thine own hands." These scriptures are awesome, but the icing on the cake is Jeremiah 1:12, which just straight out says that He watches over His Word, and He speeds things up to fulfill His promises.

NOTES

*Chapter 2*

# Stepping Up, Means Stepping Down

*Poor leaders are poor followers,*
*Great leaders are great followers*

John the Baptist, the first cousin of Jesus, made a life changing statement in the book of John chapter 3 verse 30, "He must increase, and I must decrease." This is such a powerful statement in and of itself. All steps to greatness in the Kingdom of God begin with serving and humility. James 4:6-10 says, "Humble yourselves in the sight of the Lord, and He shall lift you up." Take a look at the reason of the importance of humility before God and man. John 14 verse 12 Jesus says, "Verily, verily, I say unto you, He that believeth on Me, the works that I do shall he do also; and greater works than these shall he do, because I go unto my Father."

Knowing Jesus says this about your future, the foundation you build on has to be of the Kingdom of Heaven, or the way God wants things done. The nature of God is the missing link of success. We cannot act, think, or respond like the world to experience success in the Spirit realm as well as in the natural. Peter said to come out from amongst the world; In this he is addressing the internal issues of mindsets or patterns of response, our thought lives. The separation is not in how we dress or what we possess. But our strength is in Christ. We are not of this world, so why think or act like this world? Prepare yourself to live in the Spirit realm and in Heaven for eternity. Keep seeking God to learn His ways and power.

## "He must increase, and I must decrease."

As we fulfill the will of God in our lives, it is of major importance we have the nature of God and the Holy Spirit as our personal purpose in all our responses. Remember, "To whom much is given, much is required." There is great responsibility in the believer of Jesus Christ just based on the purpose of why Jesus came. In 1st John 3:8 the scripture tells us, "For this purpose the Son of God was manifested, that He might destroy the works of the devil."

NOTES

30

How and when you yield to the Spirit of God helps determine the outcome of many lives and situations including yours. Doing the works of Jesus, by precept and example changes lives, for you are the only Gospel that some people read. Your obedience to the call of God on your life heals the sick, encourages the hopeless, and saves souls from hell. You are needed, wanted and in great demand for the purpose of the Kingdom of God. Remember, Jesus said the harvest of souls is ready, but the individuals willing to go into the world (the harvest field) to bring them into the Kingdom of God are few. (Mathew 9:37).

## "To whom much is given, much is required."

We all have a responsibility in reaching the lost, sick and dying for Jesus. The  lives out in the world are co-dependent upon our obedience to do the work of the Holy Spirit as Jesus did. (John 14:12). You have the right and ability to follow Jesus, in all that you do. The power of the Creator of heaven and earth is in you. Sovereignty is in you. No one can make you do what you don't want to do. God is the same way. What moves God is faith in Him and His Word.

Jesus said if you want to become great in the Kingdom of God, you must be servant of all. Poor leaders are poor followers, and great leaders are great followers. A leader that has a problem

NOTES

with patience can become abusive because of their own lack of self-control in having patience and grace toward someone or something. Submission and accountability is part of authority, and balance is the hardest thing to find at times. Having relationships of conscience or friends you can trust, make a difference. Situations can be altered with just having the right people in your life.

A Roman centurion whose servant was sick told Jesus that He did not have to follow him to heal his servant; this centurion must have loved his servant to ask Jesus personally to heal him. He told Jesus to just speak the word; it is the same thing in our lives, what you say affects what you don't say. When you understand authority, you know what it takes to get things done. He knew the authority that Jesus had, so he said to just speak the word. Jesus said He had never found so great a faith in all of Israel. Meekness or humility is power under control, so is greatness power under control. Jesus could have destroyed the whole world, but He fulfilled His call and purpose in saving our lives forever. To fulfill the call of God on your life, keep in mind you are called to serve not be served.

Doing the works of Jesus, by precept and example changes lives; Humility is a key word in stepping up by stepping down; Moses called himself the meekest man on earth, and God's opinion did

NOTES

_____

_____

_____

not disagree with him. Meekness, meaning power under control, is the attribute and character needed to know when to step up into authority versus the humility of just being quiet and waiting with patience on timing. Your own self-image and how you allow or expect yourself to be treated plays a major role in how you treat others.

Remember the thumbprint of God is on you, not based on your past, but based on your future. The finished product is what has His seal of approval. The identity of how God sees you is totally different than most of us see ourselves. One, He loves you more than you can understand or know. He believes in you beyond what you are used to. He is patient with you, waiting on you to make the right choices in life that place you in the position for promotion.

## Chapter 3

# The Anointing is a way of life

In the book of Isaiah chapter 10 verse 27, the scripture tells us that the anointing destroys the yoke of bondage. Bondages can be sickness, bad habits, demonic control and influence, addictions and even emotional wounds of the past. The very presence of God is the anointing. In the presence of God the variations and manifestations of the anointing works in different ways. Psalms 16:11 tells us that in His presence is the fullness of joy. Second Corinthians 3:17 tells where the Spirit of the Lord is there is liberty and freedom. The manifestation of the Holy Spirit and the gifts of the Spirit as stated in 1st Corinthians 12 are in direct relationship with the anointing and presence of God.

First John 2:27 decrees, "But the anointing which ye have received of Him abides in you." This statement is so awesome just knowing the same Spirit that raised Jesus from the dead lives in me. Wow! Romans 8:11 tells us "But if the Spirit of Him that raised up Jesus from the dead dwells in you, He that raised up Christ from the dead shall also quicken (the word quicken, means to anoint) your mortal bodies by His Spirit that dwells in you." Then Jesus said in John 14:12 that the same works He did, I shall do also and even greater works.

The anointing is the presence of God in our lives, the ability, the grace, the power and display of the Holy Spirit in our lives. The anointing is the greatest experience on this earth. To have the Creator of the universe share and trust us with His presence and power is awesome. Isaiah 10:27 tells us that the anointing destroys the yoke of bondage in people's lives. Acts 10:38 even more tells us of Jesus and how He was anointed with the Holy Ghost, who went about doing good and healing all that were oppressed of the devil.

## The very presence of God is the anointing

We have the anointing within us and upon us at times as the Spirit of God allows based on our relationship with Him. There is a price of purity, also known as holiness. There is a price of spending time with God on a consistent daily basis. Being born again while staying washed in the blood of Jesus and keeping our mind washed by the water of the Word of God is a require-

--------------------- NOTES ---------------------

_____

_____

_____

ment. Worshipping the Lord Jesus with a continual attitude of living to please Him allows Him to use you and flow through you to minister to others. Seeking the heart of God takes time, investment of heart, mind, will and emotions.

So as we recognize what our calling and gifting's are, we still have the responsibility of humility before Him. For you to become great in the Kingdom of God, you must learn the ways of God. He wants you serving Him by serving mankind on this earth. That is just a small idea with the purpose of learning to flow in the anointing.

We have immediate access to the presence of God for us to learn His ways, so that through us He can do His mighty acts and display His love. Practice the presence of God. Lift your hands high and say, "Jesus, Jesus, Jesus." Tell Him out loud of your love for him and feel His presence come upon you.

## Every Calling has an Anointing for Ability & Purpose

My mother told me that as a little boy I would play outside till I got mad at someone and then come in the house and play Evangelist Jimmy Swaggarts record on both sides. Then I would go back outside to play again. My mother told me that I would do this about three or four times a week. Recognizing the call of

―――――――――――――― NOTES ――――――――――――――

_____

_____

_____

God upon someone's life is watching the directions of the heart. Every calling has an anointing for ability of purpose.

Some gifting's are in music, singing, playing instruments, others are a natural in math or have a desire for careers in law enforcement. The desires of our past help set the patterns of our present. Not all desires are God given when it comes to the call of God on one's life. The story of Mary and Joseph taking baby Jesus to be dedicated to the Lord in the temple says that immediately Anna the prophetess and Simeon recognized Jesus as the anointed one, the Messiah.

God knew you in your mother's womb and had a plan and purpose for your life. The hand of the Potter started working on you before you breathed your first breath. The Thumb Print of God is His seal of approval. On the Day of Judgment we that have fought the fight and kept the faith will hear, "Well done thou good and faithful servant, enter into the joy of the Lord."

God sees the finished work and knows the outcome of His investment in each individual. No, it's not predestined success or failure in our lives. God has given everyone on this earth the ability of choice. As William Shakespeare said, "To be or not to be, that is the question." Every human being has the sovereign right of recreating their past or creating their future. But if you

---

NOTES

---

keep your heart in God' hand, the anointing will help keep you in God's will. Even though God could make you do things, He did not make you a puppet or a slave. But when you got born again, you became a child of God.

## The desires of our past help set the patterns of our present

You have an assignment, a pursuit of destiny. The only question is; are you willing to pay the price of accomplishment? Going to school to be a doctor is costly in time and responsibility. The excessive price of time with the investment of knowledge assimilation requires commitment. Then the effort to help others and maintaining standards for the sake of humanity's health and wellbeing is very costly. You could say only those with the calling pay the price for excellence.

From the efforts of a mechanic to the necessity and commitment of engineers comes the designing of a better car, a bridge, a skyscraper or machinery that makes electricity. For humanity to prosper, individuals have to succeed. The calling and equipping are like breathing and exhaling. You cannot do one without the other, both are needed to live long and prosper. The anointing in the market place of this world is just as important as the anointing in building the Kingdom of God in the tabernacle or

_____ NOTES _____

_____

_____

_____

the local church. Responsibility given requires efforts made. I taught my children that "if you don't try, you have already failed." Become a seeker and you will find, Psalms 37: verses 3, 4 and 5 states, "Trust in the Lord, and do good; so shalt thou dwell in the land and verily thou shalt be fed. Delight thyself also in the Lord; and he shall give thee the desires of the heart. Commit thy way unto the Lord; trust also in him; and he shall bring it to pass". Everyone has a calling, Matthew 22:14 states "For many are called, but few are chosen." The chosen ones have made the choice to prepare for purpose in fulfilling their calling. Seek God, read His word and prepare your lifestyle for God to use you in changing lives. The Thumb Print of God fulfills the desire of the hungry.

NOTES

*Chapter 4*

# The Power of Faithfulness

Trust is a word to be earned and not lightly given. An individual's commitment in their heart is the beginning of tomorrow but is not always the outcome of the moment. Trust is a reward of faithfulness which creates a positive attitude of expectancy in giving someone influence and authority over the cherished and valued. In the book of Luke chapter 16 with verses 10-13 we find the prerequisite for leadership.

## For humanity to prosper, individuals have to succeed

"Whoever is faithful in a very little is faithful also in much; and whoever is dishonest in a very little is dishonest also in much. If then you have not been faithful with the dishonest wealth, who will entrust to you the true riches? And if you have not been faithful with what belongs to another, who will give you what is your own?"

41

Galatians 6:7 says God is not taken lightly or treated with insignificance, for what you cause to happen in your life by choices, is the future of what comes back to you. We all recreate our past or create our future by our responses and the choices we make. Luke 16:13 says, "No servant can serve two masters; for a servant will either hate the one and love the other, or be devoted to the one and despise the other."

You cannot serve God and wealth. The definition of faithfulness is "strict or thorough in the performance of duty: a faithful worker." Loyalty is the faithfulness of God to you, His will and His Word Faithfulness is "One that is true to one's word, promises, vows; an individual that is steady in allegiance or affection; loyal; constant; faithful friends. One that is reliable, trusted, or believed." If we are to be disciples of Christ and called sons of God, the resemblance should be noticed in our pursuit of life.

We, as individuals, will not be perfect all the time, even as we are being perfected during our times of test and trials as stated in Psalms 138:8. Psalms 105:19 says the word of God tried Joseph while he was in prison. Temptations come while poor spontaneous decisions are made. Mistakes happen, but faith in someone should not quit. Malachi 7:8 states, "Rejoice not against me, O mine enemy: when I fall, I shall arise; when I sit in darkness, the LORD shall be a light unto me." Proverbs 24:16 says, "A right-

_____ NOTES _____

_____

_____

_____

eous man falls seven times, but rises again." The issue is not that you fall, but do you get up. A winner never quits and a quitter never wins.

## Faithfulness is a prerequisite to promotion

James chapter one tells us that a double minded individual receives nothing from the Lord. Wow! Being double minded, means confused with the lack of commitment to do anything. There are levels of growth, but also levels of responsibility. The relationship God has with you is a commitment to see your future become your today, your tomorrow become your moment. His grace wants to be there for you even when you make a mistake, to help you overcome the past and establish His ways in your character.

A scripture in the book of Amos so clearly outlines what is taking place as circumstances challenge your life. How can two walk together, unless there is agreement? Are you committed to repeat your past or are you committed to fight to change your today? Life is a choice, to hit the snooze alarm or get up out of bed. The power of choices is like to eat healthy or not eat healthy. As Shakespeare said in Hamlet, "to be or not to be that is the question." Faithfulness is a prerequisite to promotion and maintaining a strong relationship. What you believe in is what

————————————— NOTES —————————————

_____

_____

_____

you invest in. Jesus said "No greater love has anyone, than to lay his life down for his friend," that is not just lay down my moment but my future, my desires and dreams as well.

Your level of worth has not only to do with your purpose on earth, but also your commitment to see the fulfillment of your responsibility. How you see yourself has everything to do with how you want to be seen. As God sees all and knows all He still has put His Thumb Print on you with approval based on His faith in you. He trusts you with influence in people's lives.

In First Samuel chapter 16, King Saul disobeyed God by second-guessing and leading others to do something contrary to the will of God. Obedience to instruction is a part of faithfulness. Pure obedience is done without thinking. It is never a sacrifice at the point of hearing. Obedience is a step of relational preference and commitment to the cause of Christ. Obedience to the Word of the Lord should be the unconscious action.

## What you believe in is what you invest in

I desire that God the Holy Spirit always see me as a vessel of honor; an individual who can be trusted with little or much. How can you lead where you have never been or how can you give what you do not have? This is done with an attitude of faith,

_____ NOTES _____

_____

_____

_____

a purpose of heart and an investment of time. Second Timothy 2:20 sheds some light on the vessels of honor and dishonor. These vessels are instruments for God's use. They are people with purpose and special abilities given to them by Father God. Some can sing beautifully. Some can paint and draw with skill, some are good in math and some are not. For all faithfulness is a key to unlock the future.

Some people have to study hard to pass a test, while others breeze through it. Change only happens when you add to or take something away. I want to be a vessel unto honor, one that God can trust. In the book of Acts a man named Stephen shared his knowledge, his heart and his love for the people of Jerusalem. What men gave him were stones thrown at him which killed him. Jesus gave him a standing ovation of reception as Stephen left earth and stepped into heaven. Stephen was faithful unto death.

There are vessels of gold, vessels of silver, even wood and earth. I am being changed into the image of Jesus from glory to glory by allowing His Word and Spirit to bring change inside out. God looks at your heart, while men look at your exterior. The Old Testament book of Deuteronomy has a statement that seals the deal. Verses 19 and 20 are strong statements, "I call heaven and earth to record this day against you, that I have set before all of

———————————————— NOTES ————————————————

_____

_____

_____

you life or death, blessing or cursing: therefore choose life that both thou and thy seed may live; That thou may love the LORD thy God, that thou may obey His voice, that thou may cleave unto him, for He is thy life."

We create our future with our words and actions, or we recreate our past by sometimes doing nothing. The choices we make start to take shape as we evaluate to be or not to be a doer of the Word of God. Where your heart is, displays where your future begins. Your moment is the beginning of your fulfillment. God is a Spirit and we must worship Him in Spirit and in truth. Shakespeare put it, "to thine own self be true."

Ask yourself, if you were judged right now, what would the outcome be - faithful or unfaithful? Can God trust you with your tomorrow yet? Some things we go through in our lives are nothing more than training for reigning. Being positioned for leadership begins with a faithful, trustworthy follower of Jesus who enjoys serving and leading by example.

------------------------------ NOTES ------------------------------

*Chapter 5*

# Vision, Purpose, Time

Your vision, your purpose and your time are what God uses to develop you into the person he has called you to be. Overall in life, all you have to do is decide what to do with the time given to you. The beginning of your tomorrow starts every morning before the sun comes up. Lamentations states that His mercy is new every morning. I am glad for every new day which is a second chance at life. Personally I love having my birthday because it is another year that I have conquered death.

But without goals or desires our lives are at what is called a stalemate. A stalemate is when things are not happening and it seems as if you are repeating your past. Take inventory of what you want, what you expect and what you're doing to bring about what you want and expect. Proverbs 29:18 gives a clue as to why things are not happening. "Without a vision, people perish." Faith has expectancy, expectancy has purpose and purpose is vision. A vision has borders, perimeters and guidelines.

Moses, in Hebrews 11:25-26, is listed as refusing, choosing, esteeming and forsaking all to accomplish the call and mandate of God on his life. He refused to be called the son of Pharaoh's daughter and even gave up the riches of that life. He forsook the education of Egypt's elite, the prestige and authority of Pharaoh's court while seeking out to know the God of Israel. His priorities of esteeming to know Christ, to the riches of His knowledge proved to be the most important choice Moses or anyone could make.

Realize you can never get to where you want to go without leaving where you are at presently. Vision has purpose. Identify one you have the other. If you are repeating the same cycle of life, then focus on what has not been accomplished to bring promotion. Focus is the ability to look and pursue a certain goal not giving place to distractions. Once the word of the Lord came to me and told me that if Satan could distract, He could attack. Life is full of surprises but none of them need to come from the devil. That is the purpose and reason that James tells us not to be double minded. Confusion happens when a choice is not made. Even a wrong choice is better than confusion.

NOTES

# Insanity is repetition while expecting different results

If you make a mistake, you can learn from your past and keep on going toward your future. The Father knows your weakness and your strengths. God knows what excites you and what ignites you. He knows who you are in private, whether your pillow is wet with tears or squeezed with anger. He saw you when you took your first steps and He will be there when you take your last breath. He loves you, He made you and His hand is on you. The Thumb Print can become the grip of God on your life as you allow Him to hold you and your future.

While you were in your mother's womb, He saw that you were wonderfully made. The color of your real hair, the color of your eyes, your ears, your nose and even your fingerprints He designed. You are special from beginning to end. You had nothing to say about your beginning but you have almost everything to say concerning the end of your life. Getting into agreement with God should be a committed focus on your part everyday of your life. Knowing that every breath you take could be the last one, knowing that in a moment you could be standing before God to be judged for what you did or did not do. So, live your life to the fullest.

Your identity is not what you look like on the outside, but what

————————————————— NOTES —————————————————

you look like on the inside. First Samuel 17 says God told the prophet Samuel that men look at the outward appearance, but God looks at the heart. There is not an individual on this earth that has the voiceprint that sounds like you, nor does anyone have fingerprints like yours. The iris of your eyes, if scanned with a laser, would show no other person on earth has your eye print.

## The Thumb Print can become the grip of God on your life

You are more than unique. The Potter, the creator of all creation put in you the intricate details that are only you from inside out. The one thing that makes you special in His eyes is His opinion of you, which holds the mark of years of molding, reshaping and adjusting for your days of destiny. In the book of Jeremiah, the prophet makes a statement of declaration concerning his own self but could apply to all of us on this earth. God is telling Jeremiah that, "Before I formed thee in the belly I knew thee; and before thou came forth out of the womb I sanctified thee, and I ordained thee a prophet unto the nations." The definition of the word sanctified, is to be separated with purpose. Jesus makes the same statement in John 17 about being sanctified. Jesus said that He sanctifies Himself through truth and the Word of God which is the eternal truth.

———————————————————— NOTES ————————————————————

_____

_____

_____

For Jesus and you to agree, your foundation must be the Word of God which is the Bible. It is not the teachings of Buddha or the Koran, but the Old and New Testament called the Bible. You have a specific purpose, and that purpose fulfilled is like a roll of dominos that are placed in order for one to affect the other to create the outcome. You have missed if you don't keep yourself in the will of God. Some people will not be touched or ministered to and some lives will not be changed, if you are not where God wants you in this life. Your make-up, the real you, is not just in genetics or one's blood type, but one's DNA. Your DNA should read that you have the DIVINE, NATURE, and ATTRIBUTES of God. Now that you are a new creation in Christ, you are a child of destiny. You are not only a part of the body of Christ, but a major issue for Kingdom results.

The Holy Spirit and the Father will spend years of preparation in preparing you for one moment. You may not see how important you are at this place and time, or how you will make a substantial difference in the lives of others. Remember 1st Corinthians 12 tells us that the weakest, least esteemed individuals are the choice of God with the most important purpose. As illustrated with the dominos, the chain of events in your life can put you in the right place at the right time with the right frame of mind to do the most complicated action that changes lives forever.

--------- NOTES ---------

_____

_____

_____

51

There is a law in some countries called the Law of Eminent Domain. This law is used to impose the rights of the government over individual rights. The application of the Law of Eminent Domain is stating the needs of the many, is greater than the needs of the one. That is the same thing that happened to Jesus, the needs of the many, outweighed the needs of the one. His pure and holy life was sacrificed so that every person that calls on the name of Jesus can experience the change from darkness into light.

It's like the scripture Jesus said "No greater love has anyone than this, than to lay down his life or lifestyle for his friend." Your investment of the moment could bring out the next sweeping move of God in a region. I heard Kenneth E. Hagin (Dad Hagin to all us Rhema graduates) say that it is easier for God to speed us up in His will, than correct our mistakes. Waiting on God is something you learn. It's not always what you do, but how you do it.

Patience is not a duration of time, but the frame of your mind The Holy Spirit told me once 'that the fruit of your lips comes from the seed of your thoughts." James chapter 3 tells us that your tongue can change the course of nature. The tongue can start a war or bring peace. It's like a rudder on a ship. The direction the tongue takes you is either to safe water or a rocky dan-

—————————————— NOTES ——————————————

_____

_____

_____

gerous shore. Proverbs says that life and death are in the power of the tongue. It is important that you learn the ways of the Holy Spirit and let Him set a watch over your mouth to keep you in check. If the Spirit of God cannot lead you, the devil will try to cause calamity to overtake you.

**If the devil can manipulate your emotions, he will manipulate your lifestyle!**

NOTES

*Chapter 6*

# Letting Fruit Grow

Loose lips sink ships, is an old saying that I grew up with which speaks about the power of words; Words are the beginning of all wars. It's amazing how going through hard or difficult times in one's life causes the negative words to flow out of one's mouth. Murmuring, whining, complaining seem to be the words we should fight to keep from saying as circumstances try to wear us to a frazzle. The prophet Daniel states that Satan tries to wear down the saints (Daniel 7:25), making you weary in well doing (Galatians 6:9).

## The fruit of your lips comes from the seed of your thoughts

Over a period of time being weary in well doing can be a challenge of our stability and commitment. As with all, except for the grace of God in our lives we would fall back into some type of sin. In our life there are spring, summer, autumn and winter seasons. These seasons can be as the weather around the world. For me here in the United States, winter is cold, wet and not always beautiful. There are no flowers, no fruit on trees and leaves have fallen. Life seems gray. Having an extended winter experience has a lot to do with letting our feelings rule our responses versus making my mouth line up with the Word of God. Concerning moments of despair, you must remember it's just a moment.

Life goes on and you overcome the fear, frustration, and anger as time takes place during this time when all life seems to disappear. A spring is full of life. It's like the birds singing, flowers blooming and the freshness in the air is wonderful. Spring comes with storms and with the wind blowing. But we keep going as the surrounding changes from seed time to harvest time as we are our watching gardens grow.

## An Apple tree is based on its roots, not just its fruits

Summers are the time changing element when we can anticipate the harvest in the midst of hot days. To anticipate the coming of fall there will be cool nights while the harvest is being readied to be harvested. This is for us to bring in the fruit of our labor. As summer is shifting to the falling leaves of autumn,

— NOTES —

56

inside of ourselves we know winter is on its way.

Satan tries to wear down the saints' emotions to cause frustration and fear in our seasons of life, this allowing anger to plant a seed of bitterness or doubt in God's faithfulness. Having faith in God's faithfulness and growing the fruit of the Spirit is what disappears over time if we allow our problems to stay in the sub consciousness of our minds. To bring back the pain of the mo-ment is the devil's decree. You see he does not want you to have freedom and liberty. He wants to steal your joy, your peace, your purpose and your identity in Christ. This is why Psalms 107: 2 is so important in your life. It says "Let the redeemed of the Lord say so, whom He has redeemed from the hand of the enemy."

Know this above all things, "The greater one is in you." (I John 4:4) If you have been born again, "no weapon formed against you shall prosper." (Isaiah 54:17) You overcome the enemy by the blood of the Lamb, and the word of your testimony. (Revela-tions 12:11) You can do all things through Christ, who strength-ens you (Philippians 4:13). Jesus overcame Satan in the wilder-ness with the sword of the Spirit, which is the Word of God.

When God exposed Job to Satan, the devil did not know the

_____ NOTES _____

_____

_____

_____

57

weakness of the man of God called Job. God had to have faith in Job's commitment as much as Job had to have faith in his covenant with God and Job knowing in his heart that God could not lie, but always keeps His word. In Psalms 105:17 - 19 this describes that the Word of God tried Joseph. Joseph did not prove the Word of God worked; but the opposite, the Word proved that Joseph was ready for promotion. If you will read the book of Genesis chapter 41 starting with verse 14, you will see he got a big promotion. You battles proves your commitment and integrity.

## Conflict or confrontation proves what you are made of

Conflict or confrontation proves what you are made of and how much you believe in what is in you? Do you give up easily, or hang in there and keep fighting the good fight of faith? Believing God and not believing in yourself is going in a circle of confusion. Stand in faith, agree with what the Father believes is in you. He is perfecting those things that concern you. For an apple tree is not an apple tree because of when the apples are ripe hanging on the tree, but because of the roots. The roots of one's life establish what you are, not what it looks like to others or your season of lack and despair. Seasons change so should you, as stated in II Corinthians 3:17 - 18, from glory to glory and into the very image of Christ.

——————————————— NOTES ———————————————

_____

_____

_____

## Chapter 7

# Corrections brings Perfection

Years ago while pastoring in Nashville, Tennessee, I was leaving a movie theater with my family and the voice of the Lord spoke to me these words, "I am perfecting those things that concern you." Up to that point the Spirit of God was amplifying every leaf shape and the difference between birds, bees, leaves, trees which kept me intrigued. I noticed how God colored the butterfly and stayed in the lines. His artistic ability was awesome. As I looked at the different shapes of birds, their colors and the layout of their feathers, I noticed the distinct differences of people. Each one had different shapes and sizes which was amazing to me.

I started looking at animals and distinctions between cows, horses, mules, dogs and cats. The imagination of God is so broad and expansive that it was amazing. The movie I saw dealt with the universe and its unlimited size. The stars, galaxies were humongous, all beyond my ability to comprehend. Then all at once the Spirit of God spoke to me saying, "I am perfecting what concerns you."

## Forgiveness starts out in faith

Immediately, I looked for a scripture to identify the words spoken and where the Holy Spirit was going with His statement. I found the scripture in Psalms 138 verse 8, "The LORD will perfect that which concerns me: thy mercy, O LORD, endures forever: forsake not the works of your own hands." As I meditated on the scripture the understanding came to me that what concerns me is not what happens to me as much as how I respond to what happens to me. What happens to me is God's responsibility because He is my protection and my shield. He is my rampart and strong tower, my ever-present help in time of trouble. He is my redeemer. But my response is the issue.

How I respond is up to me, to turn the other cheek and forgive them. Making myself operate in love is a matter of choice, not feelings. Love conquers all, for God is love. To act like Jesus is a matter of choice. To forgive like Jesus is a choice. Forgiveness starts out in faith. The feelings of release from the offense may take some time.

——————————————— NOTES ———————————————

_____

_____

_____

## "All it takes for evil men to triumph is for good men to do nothing."

Stepping out and being bigger than someone else's problem is an act of faith and faith works by love. How you respond is your seed which is sown toward your own future. Abraham was called the friend of God just based on the fact that Abraham believed God and this was counted to him righteousness (James 2:23). Abraham knew God personally. Spending time seeking to know God will build an unbreakable relationship with Him, His Spirit and His Word.

Everything in life has consequences. What you sow is what you reap. But there is the awesome mercy and grace of God which is new every morning as stated in Lamentations 3:22-25. In Psalms 23 the last verse says, "Surely goodness and mercy shall follow me all the days of my life." I sometimes think these are the angels that followed David cleaning up behind him. The triumph of evil is always at the expense of good. No matter what wrong King David did, God's grace and mercy was with him. God hates evil! In the 1600's a man named Edmond Burk spoke to the British Parliament and made this statement, "All it takes for evil men to triumph, is for good men to do nothing." The Apostle James said to "be doers of the Word and not hearers only."

———————————————— NOTES ————————————————

_____

_____

_____

## "The measure you seek God will be the measure that men seek you."

Jesus said His words are spirit and life. How much more should we be immersed in the Word and work of God as instructed to Joshua after Moses' death. I have a statement I apply to myself, "The measure you seek God will be the measure that men seek you." What you believe in, is what you invest in. Be pliable, be responsible, and you will see the God of the incredible. He stills works miracles today!

The only way perfection can take place is the price of testing, while looking for flaws and fallacies. Even Jesus was not perfect till he passed all the required responsibility to be the sacrificial lamb Spotless and pure. Sinless was not just about what people saw in Jesus, but what God knew about Jesus' subconscious, His thoughts and even Jesus' attitude of being willing and obedient. Remember that Jesus was the son of man as much as He was the Son of God. He overcame every test and trial that any one person could encounter in the past, present or future.

Having a life of progress requires change while working toward perfection. This requires a measure of quality, endurance for equipping for one's purpose. When you are called of God, the gifts and callings are without regret by God and for you there is

NOTES

62

no turning down what the creator of Heaven and Earth requires. Even Jesus said that whoever puts their hand to the plow and quits is not fit for the Kingdom of God (Luke 9:62). Correction of vision, or how you see things, should be a priority in keeping one's vision and assignment parallel.

When what you want does not line up with what God requires, it can create problems. Isaiah 1:19 tells of the required response to instruction. Being willing and obedient are two issues which cannot be separated. They produce the results of blessing and enjoying the good of the land as both are one in accomplishment. If you do not like correction you can never come into perfection, especially in what God requires of your response which makes you the overcomer and victor in life.

NOTES

*Chapter 8*

# The Chalice of Change

Jesus said he had to drink this cup, the cup of suffering also known as the chalice, which was the price required for change. Jesus said, "This cup shows the new agreement that God makes with His people. This new agreement begins with My blood which is poured out for you." Change never comes cheaply. Somewhere in your past, present or future there has been a price paid to institute change. Believe me change is not change, till it's changed. Your future should not be a repeat of your past. There is no repeating of the past or to say simply there is no déjà vu with what God has called you to!

Everyone has heard parts of the story of Job if they are familiar with the Bible in some form or another. It's an old story but everyone from sinner to saint knows the references of Job and his wife. Let's look at the story from an angle of faith and trust. God exposed Job to Satan, and said there was no one that was faithful like Job. God had faith in Job, now the test was could Job trust God no matter what happened in his life. During this time of battle over the will and soul of Job, who being a single individual. God sat back and watched while Satan attacked this righteous man in every area of his life.

## God has faith in you, because love believes the best

God was not worried or fretful or concerned whether Job would deny God's faithfulness. Not only did Job have to have faith and trust in God, but God had to have faith and trust in Job. Now in comparing Job to you, God is developing a trust relationship where you can trust Him and He can trust you. In the book of Job chapter 1 verses 6 - 12, we find the beginning of sorrows. The Father God exposes Job to Satan and He made the statement that there was not another man on earth like him. That same statement is made about you. It's plain and simple, there is no one like you on earth and God will not allow anything to be put on you that you cannot bear ( First Corinthians 10:13). God believes in you more than you know.

I tell people what I learned from Dad Hagin at Rhema, that you are never prepared to live till you're prepared to die. I personally would rather go to Heaven early than go to Hell late. My future

---

NOTES

---

_____

_____

_____

is in God's hands. Not that I am predestined to Heaven or Hell, but I am predestined to be like Jesus. To be like Jesus, I drink my cup of sorrows, bear the responsibility of change and know that all things work for my good according to God's purpose for my life.

The old hymn that says to "trust and obey, for there is no other way, to be happy in Jesus is to trust and obey" is an awesome song with strength and peace. Remember, your make-up in genetics is more than just blood type, but one's DNA. Your DNA should read that you have the DIVINE, NATURE, and ATTRIBUTES of God. Your identity should be based on what God thinks about you, not what your past describes. Now that you are a new creation in Christ, you are a child of destiny. You are not only a part of the body of Christ, but a major issue. Remember your fingerprints are like no one else on this earth. Your voice print, you in the natural and spiritual stand out among the millions when you have faith in God.

Even when all of Job's friends and even his own wife turned against him, Job settled it in his own heart no matter what came he took this position, " Though he slay me, yet will I trust in him." This is commitment that will guarantee you promotion and reward. To stay committed to what you know is God's will is the chalice of life. The gifts and callings are without repentance.

—————————————— NOTES ——————————————

_____

_____

_____

Second Timothy 2:19 tells me that" God knows those that are His." In ways that we don't notice the love of God is reaching out to us.

Genesis 18 describes the faithfulness of Abraham. God makes this comment about the trust He has in Abraham. "He will direct his children and children's children in the ways of the Lord, to do justice and judgment and that which is right in the sight of the Lord." The Father God knew what to expect out of Abraham. His lifestyle played a role in decisions which set the standard of trust.

Even though First Corinthians says faith and love believe the best about someone, my faith cannot make decisions for you or predict what choices you will make, unless I have understanding from the Spirit of God. You are responsible to make your own decisions in line with the will and Word of God, the Bible. There are those which use witchcraft to cause manipulation, intimidation, and control of someone's thoughts. Your choices are what the Devil wants to control. But Jesus came to give life and life more abundantly which is the ability to have excessive freedom to make good or bad choices.

Revelations 12:11 speaks prophetically that overcoming problems in life is accomplished by the sword of the Spirit, which

NOTES

is the Word of God. "They overcame the devil by the blood of the Lamb, and the word of their testimony; and they loved not their lives unto their death." Our testimony is the declaration of what we do and believe in the midst of spiritual battles that go on in our lives. The blood of Jesus separates your past from your future. This stops the devil from using your mistakes or acts of rebellion against you. The blood of Jesus helps restrict the law of sowing and reaping from being applied as judgment against you. Why? It is because the mercy of God is new every morning. First John 1:9 states "If we confess our sins, He is faithful and just to forgive us our sins, and to cleanse us from all unrighteousness." After repentance, this is what God does with your past. Repentance is not saying you're sorry, but choosing to not allow yourself the ways of life that are different from Gods standards. Psalms 103:12, "He has taken our sins away from us as far as the east is from west." The issue with God is not that you fall as much as do you get back up and try again to maintain a right relationship in holiness with Him. Holiness is not how you dress but, how you respond emotionally and mentally to conflict and situations in life. Do you act like Jesus or the world? God has His thumbprint on your life and He is still the Potter shaping us as His vessels unto honor.

---

NOTES

---

---

---

# Pure obedience is never a sacrifice

Abraham had such a good relationship with God that God shared secrets with Abraham. God came to earth to destroy two cities which lived in excessive sin and rebellion toward the ways of God. These two cities were called Sodom and Gomorrah. Sin is an attitude of the heart and actions of the flesh that the devil uses to separate you from God and His love for you. Even if you're in church and you call yourself a Christian, you can yield to the nature of your flesh and this world to resist the ways of your creator and keep sin in your life, like unforgiveness or bitterness, murder, adultery. These can keep you out of the presence of God throughout eternity, and that means going to hell. There was a short story of a man in Genesis called Enoch. It is said that Enoch walked with God and God took him. He didn't die, but just disappeared. God took him to heaven without Enoch seeing death. This happened to Enoch because he found favor in God's eyes. What happened to Enoch will happen to us is based on our relationship with Jesus and His word. He will come to take people to heaven, which have been doing His will from their heart.

Hebrews 11:5 says "Faith enabled Enoch to be taken instead of dying. No one could find him, because God had taken him. But, before Enoch was taken, God was pleased with him."

───────────────── NOTES ─────────────────

_____

_____

_____

Even if your life or your walk with God has not been perfect, you will find that God, the Potter, is still working on you without you even knowing it. You have been bought with the precious blood of Jesus Christ. Know this that "He that begun a good work in you will perform it until the day of Jesus Christ, in this have confidence." (Philippians 1:6). Then in Philippians 2:13 the scripture says, "For it is God which works in you both to will and to do of His good pleasure." The Potter is still going to put his Thumb Print on your life if you let Him. To drink the cup of Christ, the chalice of life, commitment is obedience fulfilled. Pure obedience is never a sacrifice.

NOTES

_____

_____

_____

*Chapter 9*

# Had a Painful Past, Now a Celebrated Future

There was a woman named Ruth in the genealogy of Jesus that used to sacrifice baby blood to the Moab god named Chemosh, who seemed to have had a taste for blood. In 2 Kings 3:27 we find that human sacrifice was part of the rites of Chemosh. There was a woman named Ruth who being a priestess serv-ing Chemosh offered human sacrifices of live babies as part of their worship. Moab was a nation that was born out of incest between Lot and one of his daughters. Lot's two daughters got him drunk after they left Sodom and Gomorrah and had inter-course with Lot with intention of getting pregnant. This brought the nation of Moab and the Ammon and the man created gods called Molech and Chemosh. This is the foundation of the tribe nations of the Moabites and the Amalekites.

Even though God took Lot and his daughters out of Sodom and Gomorrah, God did not take Sodom and Gomorrah out of them. Remember Lot's wife who turned to a pillar of salt as she turned to see the destruction of the cities she loved? All of us have the potential to allow the thoughts of our past to direct our steps toward a future that might not be God's best for us. That is why reading and studying God's Word is the answer to all life's problems. Psalms One tells us not to keep company with ungodly people who don't have a relationship with Jesus.

The book of Peter says to come out from amongst the people and culture of the world. First Corinthians ask us what fellowship does light have with darkness or Christ with Belial (the world's system). Then in James 4:4 He says "You adulterous people, don't you know that friendship with the world is hatred toward God? Anyone who chooses to be a friend of the world becomes an enemy of God." These scriptures can make you confused in application. How can you be a light in the midst of darkness or as Jesus, be a friend of sinners? This is all about purity. Only the pure in heart can see God. The difference is the spirit of the antichrist spirit. Never change for the thoughts of others, only please the thoughts of God (Jeremiah 29:11).

—————————————  NOTES  —————————————

_____

_____

_____

# Being Ungodly is a matter of the heart

Ungodly people are not just someone in the world or that are out of church, there are ungodly people in churches all over the world. Ungodly status is a matter of the heart. There is no love for the Word of God or Spirit of God. You cannot have a rela-tionship with the Holy Spirit and live in sin. Sin is that which is contrary to God's Word and will. They are people that live for themselves and not the desires of Jesus, the one that gave His life for them. Lot was the nephew of Abraham. He knew the ways of God, but chose to live amongst the vilest of sinners in Sodom and Gomorrah.

The grandsons and son of Lot was the beginning of the people called Moab and the Amalekites from Ammon. The Moabites and Amalekites were known for taking babies as sacrifices to their man made gods called Molech and Chemosh. A great grandmother of Jesus was a high priestess in Moab that took babies as sacrifices to a demon god. Her name was Ruth, but Ruth changed her way of thinking and committed to the God of Israel called Jehovah. Remember the fruit of your lips is from the seed of your thoughts. Even King Solomon made God Jehovah mad at him by his actions in I Kings 11:7 Then did Solomon build an high place for Chemosh, the abomination of Moab, in the hill that is before Jerusalem, and for Molech, the abomination

_____ NOTES _____

_____

_____

_____

of the children of Ammon. The powers of darkness work to get us to compromise standards of the heart to please people rather than our creator.

Ruth, a widow, went into covenant with her mother-in-law and this opened the door of this widowed woman named Ruth to re-marry a Jew who was the grandfather of King David which is the family lineage of Jesus Christ. There is a paraphrase of Romans 12:2 that simply goes like this, "Whatever you do, do not copy the lives or habits of others. But let the Father lead you by His Spirit and He will change the very root of your life." Jesus said in John 15:3, "My words will clean you and make you whole." Even though Ruth had a dirty past, God turned things around for her because she left her past and took hold of the God of Abraham and His Word. God had His Thumbprint on her for the foundation of the birth of His Son, Jesus Christ.

## God has His thumbprint on you

Ruth made a commitment with a statement to Naomi her moth-er-in-law, "Your people will be my people, and your God will be my God." With repentance from her, God forgave her of her past. Another woman named Rahab was a major help in Israel defeating the city of Jericho. The thing is Rahab was a harlot or what we call a prostitute but she was also a great, great, grand-

---

NOTES

---

mother to Jesus. King David is stated to be a man after God's own heart. You can see that David was a murderer, an adulterer and even a liar. God loved David like He loves you. He forgave David and let King David stay in authority as the leader of God's chosen people.

There was a man named Hosea, a prophet that God told to marry a prostitute named Gomer. This man's wife kept selling herself while the man of God spoke the word of the Lord to the people. God knows details and has final say. Remember what you compromise to get, you ultimately lose.

A man of God called Jonah was given instruction by the Spirit of God. He chose not to obey the word of the Lord and was swallowed up by a fish known as a whale. This caused him to finally obey the will of God. Jonah knew God so well that he knew that his assignment required God's involvement. The whale was just an action of God to equip Jonah to fulfill his assignment. Jonah is the example Jesus uses regarding His death and resurrection. Jonah was in the belly of the well for three days like Jesus was in the heart of the earth for three days before His resurrection.

Second Corinthians tells us in chapter one that God uses the foolish things to confound the wise, the weak things to confound the strong. God's ways are different than what we want to be-

NOTES

_____

_____

_____

lieve. His ways are perfect. He works from inside out, not outside in. He works on your heart, mind and will to mold you as the Potter molds the clay into what He wants you to be.

There was a businessman named Peter who was successful and committed to what his family had done for years, fishing. A man named Jesus walked by and said two words, "Follow Me." Those two words changed Peter's life forever. All Jesus said was "Follow Me." When Peter heard those words, he left a boat full of fish in the hot sun to spoil. He left wife and children, Peter forsook all and followed Jesus. By all appearances, Peter looked irresponsi-ble to his business and family.

At one time Jesus called Peter a name that meant reed blowing in the wind. This has all the connotations of Simon being one that is inconsistent. Simon was what he was, but Jesus changed Simon to Peter which meant rock solid. God had His thumb-print on Peter and all others from the beginning of time. Even today, God has His hand on your life and when you get to Heav-en there will be a God selected new name for you to fit your eternity.

## God works from inside out, not outside in

Your past is over; and your future begins without end. So let

NOTES

_____

_____

_____

Jesus come into hidden areas of your heart and heal you from how you were treated when you were young or during troubled times in your life. Things you have gone through which are the hidden painful memories of your past. Let the Master Potter put His love for you to work reshaping your life for success, joy, peace and happiness. Jesus prophesied to Simon that God was going to make him strong and unmovable when Jesus called him Peter. Abraham's name was Abram which meant fatherless one. Then Jehovah changed Abram to Abraham which means father of many. His wife was called Sarai, **meaning** contention. So, God changed her name to Sarah which means princess.

Revelations 2:17 tells us that God will give us a new name when we get to Heaven. This new name is the declaration throughout eternity of how God sees you and how the Potter shaped you during your life on earth. You have a real Father's love, no matter what your past says about you. No matter what you have done, God loves you. If you will let the blood of Jesus cover you and allow the Holy Spirit to fill you with His power, your life will never be the same.

Peter was in some ways no different than Judas. Judas sold Jesus for 30 pieces of silver. Peter denied Jesus, cursed Jesus and just a few hours earlier, Peter the rock was strong. But Jesus prayed for Peter that his faith would not fail. Jesus prays for you and all the

NOTES

_____

_____

_____

79

people of this earth. Hebrews 7:25 says, "Jesus ever lives to make intercession for us, to save us to the utmost." But because of the temptation of Satan toward Peter, he became the reed blowing in the wind for a moment. We all have moments of being moved by what is around us rather than what is inside of us. But God controls time as stated in Acts 1:7. He has all the time in the world. So after your moment of failure, get up and ask Jesus to forgive you.

Your life is never over till God says so and right now you are reading this book and God is dealing with your heart. Let the Potter put His hand back on you or even make some changes within you. For it's His desire for you to be like Him. He wants you to be a creation of something new, your future and not recreating your past. You cannot find anyone better to be like than Jesus. For you see, "No greater love, has anyone than to lay their life down for others." Give Jesus what He gave you, your life, your future, and He will forgive your past.

Jesus knew how to restore Peter and give hope to the rest of the disciples after His death. They had yet to process His resurrection. But Jesus met them where they were, back in the boat fishing. He gave them increase in their lives with a large catch of fish and fed them while He instructed them. Relationship is investment. Take time to sit under the teacher the Holy Spirit and

---

NOTES

---


---


---

80

let Him teach you the words of life. Peter needed to forgive himself, so Jesus asks Peter in John 21, Peter do you love me? Jesus touched the depths of Peter's heart. The hurt he felt was because he let Jesus down. Three times Jesus pulled out of Peter what Peter wanted, which was to express his love for Jesus.

This question and answer moment healed Peter beyond his shame of denial. All Jesus did is asked Peter if he loved Him three times, because it was three times that Peter denied Christ. After each answer Jesus told Peter to feed His followers. Remember no matter what you have done or will do, if you will ask Jesus to forgive you and in faith receive forgiveness (1st John 1:9), Jesus will cover your past with His blood. That means in God's eyes you have no past to judge for you are forgiven. Jesus paid the price and penalty for your salvation. Salvation has three corresponding actions, saved from your past, allowed in the presence of God to learn His ways and you receive the power of the Holy Spirit to do His will.

Salvation is access to God, learning His ways and doing His acts Another individual is Paul the Apostle who at one time was called Saul of Tarsus. He was a self-appointed persecutor and extinguisher of Christians. He thought he was doing God a service by killing the followers of Jesus Christ. But Jesus saw this man's future and met him as he was going to another town to

NOTES

_____

_____

_____

search out Christians to kill them and put some in prison. When Jesus met Paul, Jesus asked the question of why Paul was trying to persecute Him. See what you do to other Christians you are doing also to Jesus, for we are the body of Christ. Jesus changed Paul's life forever. Paul called himself the greatest sinner, but the Father called him to write the majority of books in the New Testament.

The Father God will take the small things to confound the mighty, and the foolish things to confound the wise. God's ways are somewhat different than we are used to. For you to have victory over the works of the Devil, you need to learn the Word of God and speak the same things that Jesus is saying about you. Your words are the sword of the Spirit, which is the Word of God. Speaking the Words of God is the same thing that Jesus did in the wilderness when He rebuked Satan saying, "It is written Satan, get behind Me." These two statements are what came out of Jesus' mouth to overcome temptation and defeat the Devil. If there is any doubt that God can change your life just realize that you are still alive based upon the faith of our Lord Jesus Christ. He sees your future and wants you to know Him and learn His ways. His precious Holy Spirit will lead you in the path of righteousness for His name sake.

———————————— NOTES ————————————

_____

_____

_____

*Chapter 10*

# The Gifts' and Callings' Mandated Purpose

Many people like you have been called of God to represent Him and fulfill His will and purpose for your life. Jesus made the statement that the field (field representing people's souls) is ready for harvest, but the laborers are few. The call is not God calling you to a location as much as a place in grace and relationship. It is a gift which has been put inside you from God as a gift to the people of God for the work of the Kingdom of God. Not all are called to preach behind a pulpit but to share Jesus in various ways in our lives.

## What is important is not a title, but a purpose

There are people that are called to operate in the office of

Teacher, Pastor, Evangelist, Prophet and Apostle. But these offices and functions may not be directly or indirectly to working in or through a local church. You may be a CEO of a business or nurse in a hospital, a teacher in a public school or even a political figure in local, state or even national influence. Callings can range from a real-estate agent to an individual behind the counter in a convenience store.

Ephesians 4:11 is all about the development of leaders, leading by example, working together for the furtherance of the gospel of Jesus Christ. It's like your hand, the thumb is the Apostle, the Prophet is the pointing finger, the Evangelist is the finger that reaches out the furtherance, the Pastor is the ring finger that touches the heart, and the little finger is the Teacher that can open a stopped up ear. Most people look at church government being only over a building with people, but church government is spiritual and it is worldwide relational kingdom business.

## Church government is relational Kingdom influence

Recently I was driving down Hwy 96 outside of Franklin Tennessee. I saw a For Sale sign which caught my attention. I then heard the voice of the Lord saying to me "Let's take a walk." At the time I was desperate to hear from God. I went through a season of seven years that the bottom dropped out and all hell was

―――――――――――――――― NOTES ――――――――――――――――

_____

_____

_____

84

jumping up and down on me to make it go further it seemed. It was so bad the thought crossed my mind that my new name in Glory was going to be Esau, even though there was no sin in my life, it seemed God hated me. Romans 9 says, "Jacob I have loved and Esau I have hated." I had to fight with all that was in me to believe that God loved me. It's like I got the hell beat out of me so God could bring forth more heaven.

As I drove to the back of the property that was For Sale I stopped at a creek and began to walk and listen. As I was sitting on a log looking at the water flow over the rocks, I noticed moss on some of the rocks with caterpillars crawling around everywhere. As I followed the rocks in my mind, looking for steps to stand on to follow the creek the voice of the Lord came and said "Everything has purpose." I stopped walking and sat down to listen. He told me everything going on in my life had purpose.

Just like the rocks in the creek allowed the water to flow, it also created a sound of bubbling water flowing resulting in an atmosphere of peace and harmony. He told me to trust Him. At that point I wanted out of the battle, even though I loved the ministry. The pressure was at times too much. I ministered in large churches and small, having results of miracles, healings for the people. But time and again I went home with love offerings that could not pay my basic bills.

_____ NOTES _____

_____

_____

_____

I had loving, unspiritual people telling me that Paul made tents. But they knew not the voice of the Lord for me. Their words were critical, doubtful and agreeing with the lies of hell, meaning they had no faith in me. There was no voice of encouragement and they were defiantly making the choice not to invest in me. Winter for a fruit tree is winter for all, but the harvest is in the root. No matter what is on the outside of a person, what is on the inside of one's heart is what counts. Samuel was looking for a king for Israel, but God was looking for a man after His own heart.

## Your harvest is in your heart, where the Thumb print is

In First Samuel 16 God told **Samuel**, men look at appearance, but God looks at the heart. Your calling matures before your harvest. Your harvest is for others and your maturity is for you. So as the brook babbled, the caterpillars crawled, I wept knowing that purpose was working in me His good, acceptable, and  perfect will in my life. To succeed in public is wonderful, but to fail in private is hideous. You need people in your life for balance that will speak the word of the Lord no matter what is going on. I have had friends, pastors, prophets **call** me sometimes four times a week to check on me.

Then my world all fell apart.  The mother of my children filed

———————————————— NOTES ————————————

_____

_____

_____

for divorce and I was stuck obeying God or getting bitter. My friends became strangers and strangers became my friends. I saw the non-church goer invite me to Thanksgiving dinner and the people that I pastored or even ministers I knew it seemed they didn't care if I was homeless or suicidal even though I wasn't. I was to preach about trusting God, but I found myself question-ing my trust and wondering what did I do to deserve this collapse of my life. But I encouraged myself and committed with this one statement, "If I can trust Him with my eternity, why can't I trust Him with my today."

## Mistakes can be diverted, if you will seek wisdom

Purpose is the fulfillment of training. Psalms 105:19 tells the Word of the Lord tried Joseph. Before God can trust you with much, can you be faithful with little? Success can destroy you faster than failure. We need spiritual sons, but we need respon-sible Fathers to speak and guide the spiritual sons through the valley of the shadow of death. To have the relationship of trust they must know the care given was from the heart.

Mistakes can be diverted, if you will seek wisdom in the aged, the experienced ones. I mean those that have prayer lives and experience and testimonies of victory. Advice is cheap to those who don't pray, but those that have prayer lives can say look at

—————————— NOTES ——————————

_____

_____

_____

_____

the scars of victory. Confrontation produces what you are made of. Kenneth Hagin Sr. said that "It is easier for God to speed you up, than to correct your mistakes."

The perfecting of the saints is in the correcting of the saints or as stated in Ephesians 4 the equipping of the saints. No one has it all together, we are all co-dependent on the whole body of Christ. As 1st Corinthians 12 states the hand cannot say to the foot, I have no need or you. We need each other, two is stronger than one and peace is the strength of unity as well as unity is the strength of peace. The motivation and encouragement from leaders that have been where you are going helps shorten the distance. A place of maturity is a place of responsibility. **You are responsible in building a relationship as well as responding.**

The scripture in Luke 11:9 tells us to seek that we may find, ask that we might be given, knock that the door may be opened. There are some things in life that are not free. Effort is your responsibil-ity and responsibility is you responding according to your ability. Patience is the control of your response (your attitude) during a period of time, contrary to the actions that are expected. Having the strength of patience is not just a duration of time, but it is an attitude, a state of your mind. Poor leaders are impatient which allows frustration and strife taken out on others.

———————————— NOTES ————————————

_____

_____

_____

_____

# The eye gate, ear gate, or the mouth bridge

In First Corinthians 15:33 the prophet tells us "Be not deceived: evil communications corrupt good standards." It should be one of your greatest goals in life to protect your relationship with the Holy Spirit. To grieve the Holy Spirit is to do the things that He Himself has warned you not to do, speak, or look at. The eye gate, ear gate, or the mouth bridge, all functions have more to offer than just communicating on this earth. The spirit realm is more real than the natural realm. The Holy Spirit is a person so pure. He cannot tolerate things that mock His presence or attitudes of strife or un-forgiveness.

Keep yourself away from things, people and communications that grieve the precious Holy Spirit or frustrate the grace of God. He hates strife. He loves peace. He craves unity and oneness. Allow the Spirit of God to teach you the ways of God. God is love, Jesus is the Prince of Peace and the Holy Spirit is called the comforter.

There is no room for un-forgiveness or anger in His presence or in your life. The Spirit of faith is in you and faith works by love and God is love. Love believes the best, endures long, and takes no account of wrong done to it (I Cor. 13:4 Amplified Bible. Faith is what pleases God. Being a doer of His Word is living

NOTES

---

89

what He said. Being made one with God is becoming one with His Word. Faith comes from hearing the Word of God (Romans 10:17). Keep your expectancy in agreement with the Word of God. Allow yourself the time to meditate and study the Bible. As you breathe, so should you pursue the Words of Life. Become addicted to the Word of God.

Just because you go to church does not make you a Christian, just like you being in a hospital does not make you a patient, doctor or nurse. Even if God uses you with signs and wonders, this does not mean you are pleasing God. Matthew 7:21 speaks of those that have miracles, but still do not have a relationship with Jesus. Even though God is merciful, kind and slow to anger, He still is a Father that requires obedience out of His children. Just because you go to church does not make you a Christian.

You will always have the right of choice, like Shakespeare says, "To be or not to be, that is the question." God will never take away your choice Victor Frankle stated in a World War II prison camp concerning the Germans, "They can take my freedom of where I eat, sleep or work, but they cannot take away the freedom of how I choose to think." Great men and women like George Washington or Abraham Lincoln to Florence Nightin-gale all had a relationship with the Word and Spirit of God and God Himself.

—————————————— NOTES ——————————————

_____

_____

_____

In Matthew 25 the story is told of five wise and five foolish virgins. The five wise used common sense in preparation for the coming of the bridegroom. They stored up extra oil for their lamps to burn during the night of waiting. The foolish assumed they had enough to last during the whole of the night. Well guess who came up short? You see, what you take for granted can be taken from you. Wisdom is known by her children. Do not take your calling, your relationship with the Holy Spirit or your knowledge of the Word of God for- granted. The enemy sneaks in as the guard doses off the sleep. The shadow of your life falls on others. Those that you do not know are watching and following your lead and example. None of us ever want to hear Jesus say "Depart from me for I never knew you." In plain common words, Jesus is saying we never had a relationship or you only spent time with Me to get something, not know Me. These words would be hard to hear from Jesus.

Even as you read and I speak to your heart, Jesus is praying for you. Jesus is the author and finisher of your faith. He is the beginning and the end, Jesus is the Alpha and Omega, the first and the last. The foolish virgins may have had an overwhelming desire to see the wedding but did not use wisdom and responsibility in consideration of the unpredictable happening. The simple truth is you cannot be too prepared to meet God. Live every day as if it is judgment day.

———————————————— NOTES ————————————————

_____

_____

_____

# You are the thumbprint of God

You are the thumbprint of God, in His eyes of faith you are the finished vessel, but He still allows you the final say in your tomorrow, allowing you to have sovereignty and the freedom of choice. Even though the prophet Jeremiah said "shall the clay tell the potter how to shape it" the weakness of God is His love for you. (I Corinthians 1:25). If you can trust God with your eternity, why not trust Him with your today. In Psalms 66 and Jeremiah 5 both books tell us that God withholds things from us because of secret sins.

Those things are like thoughts and actions done in secret that no one knows, except you and the Holy Spirit. The Holy Spirit is the one who looks and finds people of tomorrow. Second Chronicles 16:9 tells us the eyes of the Lord are running to and fro looking for those who have set their hearts perfect toward God. That verse means those  whose hearts are set upon the Lord, their lives are to build a future in their eyes of faith and those that are living  holy as the instruction of the Lord leads them in the path of righteousness.  Those who have learned from their past the ways of God bring thought provoking of yester-year dreams which have faded away. The Holy Spirit is a reminder of destiny with expectancy for you are a person of authority with God given ability.

———————————————— NOTES ————————————————

_____

_____

_____

We all have a wonderful future in front of us. Growing and flowing with the Holy Spirit is going to be awesome and fun. Letting the love and power of God flow through us as vessels of honor which He can pour through is beyond description. The Creator using us to change lives of others is awesome. Jesus is the light of the world and when the light is on, things hidden are seen. Put everything in your past under the blood and know that God's hand is molding your future as a potter slowly shapes the outcome of His masterpiece, then He finishes it off with His thumbprint. You have the mark of God on you, even if He is still working on you. Even if it looks hopeless, have hope and faith in God, He believes in you. He loves you.

Philippians 1: 6 tells us "I'm convinced that God, who began this good work in you, will carry it through to completion on the day of Christ Jesus" (GWT). God has put the Holy Spirit in you to assist you in all that you do. Philippians 4:13 tells us "I can do all things through Christ who will enable me." I John chapter 4 talks of people that carry the Spirit of the Antichrist, but verse 4 talks directly to those whose heart is made perfect in seeking God.; "Ye are of God, little children, and have overcome them in the world: because greater is He that is in you, than he that is in the world."

Then in I John 5 even a stronger encouragement is stated, "For

—————————————————— NOTES ——————————————————

_____

_____

_____

whatsoever is born of God overcomes the world: and this is the victory that overcomes the world, even our faith. Who is he that overcomes the world, but he that believeth that Jesus is the Son of God?" The secret things in the Word of God is the understanding when you know what God knows and loves like God loves. It is a guarantee of heaven, God cannot lie. So, know this that nothing can separate you from God's faithfulness and His love for you.

Romans 8:27-39, 9:1 "26(1-26?) "And the Holy Spirit helps us in our distress, even when we do not know what we should pray for, nor how we should pray. The Holy Spirit prays in us with groaning's that cannot be expressed in words. But, the Father who knows our hearts knows what our spirit is saying. The Holy Spirit pleads for us believers by praying in harmony and agreement with God's will in us. We know that God causes everything to work together for the good of those who love God and are called according to His purpose and plan." The potter is shaping the clay and captivating our will to bless us with knowledge.

The standard of your heart should be, "If God is for us, who can ever be against us? Since God did not spare even his own Son but gave him up for us all, won't God, who gave us Christ, also give us everything else? Who dares accuse us whom God has chosen for His own will and purpose? Will God? No! He is the

---

NOTES ————

_____

_____

_____

one who has given us right standing with Himself. Who then will condemn us? Will Christ Jesus? No, for He is the one who died for us and was raised to life for us and is sitting at the place of highest honor next to God, pleading for us.

Can anything ever separate us from God's love? Does it mean He no longer loves us if we have trouble or calamity, or are persecuted, or are hungry or cold or in danger or threatened with death? (Even the Scriptures say, "For your sake we are killed every day; we are being slaughtered like sheep.") No, despite all these things, overwhelming victory is ours through Christ Jesus, who loved us.

And I am convinced that nothing can ever separate us from His love, death can't, life can't, the angels can't, and the demons can't. Our fears for today, our worries about tomorrow, and even the powers of hell can't keep God's love away. Whether we are high above the sky or in the deepest ocean, nothing in all creation will ever be able to separate us from the love of God that is revealed in Christ Jesus our Lord. Romans 9:1 Paul writes, "In the presence of Christ, I speak with utter truthfulness–I do not lie–and my conscience and the Holy Spirit confirm that what I am saying is true."

What God says about you is endless! You have the Thumbprint of God on you and His Thumbprint is like you are smothered in kisses. Take time to read this book again and listen to what I am

NOTES

_____

_____

_____

not saying as you listen to what is said. Revelatory knowledge is seeing beyond one precept at a time, read in between the lines. Then pass this on to others while allowing the seed of change to begin every morning when you wake up.

Change your today, while creating tomorrow. Speak what God says and let the fruit of your lips come from the seed of your thoughts. You are one of the best investments you could ever make in your lifetime. Remember that what you feed grows and what you starve dies. You are the Thumbprint of God. Let Him finish His work in you; seek Him as He is seeking you. You are the thumbprint of God.

1 John 5:14-15 "And this is the confidence (the assurance, the privilege of boldness) which we have in Him: [we are sure] that if we ask anything (make any request) according to His will (in agreement with His own plan), He listens to and hears us. And if (since) we [positively] know that He listens to us in whatever we ask, we also know [with settled and absolute knowledge] that we have [granted us as our present possessions] the requests made of Him." (AMP)

For you the reader, the end is only the beginning of something greater!

—————————————— NOTES ——————————————
_____

_____

_____

# Meditate the following scriptures:

Psalms 139 "O LORD, you have examined me, and you know me. You alone know when I sit down and when I get up. You read my thoughts from far away. You watch me when I travel and when I rest. You are familiar with all my ways. Even before there is a <single> word on my tongue, you know all about it, LORD. You are all around me--in front of me and in back of me. You lay your hand on me. Such knowledge is beyond my grasp. It is so high I cannot reach it. Where can I go <to get away> from your Spirit? Where can I run <to get away> from You? If I go up to heaven, You are there. If I make my bed in hell, You are there. If I climb upward on the rays of the morning sun <or> land on the most distant shore of the sea where the sun sets, even there Your hand would guide me and Your right hand would hold on to me. If I say, "Let the darkness hide me and let the light around me turn into night," even the darkness is not too dark for You. Night is as bright as day. Darkness and light are the same <to you>. You alone created my inner being. You knitted me together inside my mother. I will give thanks to You because I have been so amazingly and miraculously made. Your works are miraculous, and my soul is fully aware of this. My bones were not hidden from You when I was being made in secret, when I was being skillfully woven in an underground workshop. Your eyes saw me when I was only a fetus. Every day <of my life> was

───────────────── NOTES ─────────────────

_____

_____

_____

_____

recorded in Your book before one of them had taken place. How precious are Your thoughts concerning me, O God! How vast in number they are! If I try to count them, there would be more of them than there are grains of sand. When I wake up, I am still with you. I wish that You would kill wicked people, O God, and that bloodthirsty people would leave me alone. They say wicked things about You. Your enemies misuse your name. Shouldn't I hate those who hate You, O LORD? Shouldn't I be disgusted with those who attack You? I hate them with all my heart. They have become my enemies. Examine me, O God, and know my mind. Test me, and know my thoughts. See whether I am on an evil path. Then lead me on the everlasting path (GWT)."

Isaiah 64:8 "But now, LORD, You are our Father. We are the clay, and You are our potter. We are the work of Your hands."(GWT) Romans 9:21 "A potter has the right to do whatever he wants with his clay. He can make something for a special occasion or something for everyday use from the same lump of clay." (GWT)

For those of you that desire to come closer to Jesus, simply say these words from your heart. "Lord Jesus, **cleanse** me with your blood, forgive me of my sins. Help me Jesus to forgive others, because You forgave me. Open my eyes to Your Word to see how You lived and loved and to know that I can live for You and love like You. Be my Lord and Savior right now. I know that

————————————— NOTES —————————————

_____

_____

_____

You died for my sins and God raised You from the dead. Thank You for saving me, now heal me of all that affects my choices, In Jesus name, Amen."

Romans 10:9-10 "For if you confess with your mouth that Jesus is Lord and believe in your heart that God raised him from the dead, you will be saved. For it is by believing in your heart that you are made right with God, and it is by confessing with your mouth that you are saved."

Biography of Dr. Mark D. White
Expressing the Fathers Heart

Mark D. White was raised an Assembly of God pastor's son and started preaching at the age of 15. In 1978 he graduated from Kenneth E. Hagin's Rhema Bible Training Center in Tulsa, Oklahoma. Since then he has been an associate pastor of two churches, and has pastored three. Mark also holds a Doctorate from Saint Thomas University and a BS/BM from University of Phoenix. Mark is on the leadership team of Global Fire Ministries in Murfreesboro, Tn. with Jeff Jansen as team leader.

Mark travels extensively throughout the United States and travels International ministering the Word of God by precept and example. Having over 43 years active experience in ministry, gives place to the workings of the Holy Spirit in the lives of the believers and unbelievers. Mark's insight and practical understanding in the spirit makes room for him to operate in the Prophets' office with a pastor's heart. There is a strong tangible anointing upon him, which gives place to the open move of the Holy Spirit in edifying and comforting the local church.

Mark has a reputation for balanced teaching and preaching with compassion for the heart of the people. Homes are restored, blind eyes are opened, deaf ears are healed, cancers disappears, cataracts removed, and broken hearts are mended. The Word of God is preached with signs following. Miracles and Healings happen in every service. It is Marks desire to serve the purpose of each and every local church and ministry. Mark has written two books "Your Identity; The Thumbprint of God" and "Time the Unfound Friend."

www.markwhite.tv
Email address - rapha@gmx.us